A DAY WITH A CEO

HANDBOOK

BRIAN MOORE

WHY *THIS* BOOK?

This book has been created as a result of several decades of General Management experience covering many companies in different industries predominantly in the USA, Europe and Asia. The companies have been of varying size ranging from small family businesses to publicly traded companies. Most of this experience has been gained as a group CEO directly leading a central team and overseeing the Profit and Loss performance of many subsidiary company teams running stand-alone businesses.

The paradox is that as my career progressed, life became more complicated and the data bank of experience increased, the basic requirements of the General Management role appeared to be much simpler. The need to keep focused on basic questions and the need to keep asking *WHY ARE YOU DOING THAT?* became more relevant. *A key task of the top Executives in any organization is to simplify complex subjects for the team to understand and run with.* I hope that this comes across in this book.

The intent of the book is to cover what you require to know coupled with some very basic concepts of what is behind most management activity and some practical experience to help with your thought processes. Very few subjects are covered in depth and any further knowledge can be readily obtained from a multitude of sources. Above all the objective is to communicate *What I think you need to know* in order to be an effective General Manager (GM).

This is the first book in what is planned to be a series of *A Day With a CEO* books that scope out the job function of a General Manager. Subsequent books will focus on *Finance, People* and *Business Problems*.

Although targeted at General Managers, the content will be of use to anyone interested in how a business should be managed, especially early career managers with aspirations to become a General Manager.

Enjoy the book and remember two things — *CASH is KING* and keep asking *WHY?*

Usually there is a whole army of people around you that can manage the clever stuff!

This is the book that I wish that I had at the start of my career to act as a Road Map.
I would certainly still be carrying it with me.

ACKNOWLEDGMENTS

A special thanks to Patrick Harlington for his help, support and encouragement and his contribution in the negotiating section. Also, thank you to Michelle Jeffrey for supporting me with the development of the finance sections and helping with presenting the material.

This starts and finishes with YOU!

YOU !

This book is about you and your personal development. It is intended to make you think about the role of General Management in a BUSINESS organization and how it applies to you and your performance.

The book is full of opinions and experiences; some will work for you, some will not. Some will work some of the time, some will not. This is the nature of life and dealing with people in particular.

Leading a business organization is largely an interpersonal process, so any skills which you can develop to become better at dealing with relationships and developing your skill set to influence and inspire other people the better.

Take from this book what you want to make you a more effective manager and leader.

You are ultimately responsible for your own personal development, make a good job of it!

KNOW YOURSELF

Leadership Style / Learning Style / Myers Briggs /
Best Time of Day / Strengths and Weaknesses
Psychometric Tests / Negotiating Style

ABOUT THIS BOOK

PERSPECTIVE

This is a check list driven book taken from the perspective of the top Executive in a BUSINESS organization who reports to a governing body, typically a Board of Directors, or maybe the owner of the business. It looks at the various aspects and component parts of a business from this top position and is intended to position these activities within the context of the total organization.

The focus is on downward management and does not cover the many, and very important, upward organizations, including Boards, regulatory bodies, Governments etc., which are a growing and important part of a CEO's role.

SIMPLICITY

I make no apologies for what is hopefully a very simple book with some fairly complex subjects presented as simple messages. A key role of a GM is to analyze complex situations and to turn them into simple tasks that everyone can understand, particularly those who have to do them.

REPETITION

Many of the ideas in this book are reinforced through repetition. Any experienced Executive will tell you "People listen, but they do not hear. They will hear, but they do not understand."

Constant repetition is a requirement of most leaders.

I have read countless books of great complexity that have been built around a few simple concepts that have stood the test of time and WORK. Hopefully you will find many of them in this book and save yourself one hell of a lot of reading.

A COUPLE OF PHILOSOPHICAL POINTS

WHY THE MOUNTAIN?

Maybe a metaphor for the business journey.

An objective to reach the top?

Climbing is best done with a team.

Beware of the prevailing conditions.

The view is different depending where you are.

Be prepared for the journey, take safety equipment.

However, too much weight of equipment and that will pose a risk. Assess what is required.

It is different coming down than going up. Most accidents happen coming down!

A QUOTE FROM VOLTAIRE CIRCA 1700

"Each player must accept the cards life deals him or her: but once they are in hand, he or she alone must decide how to play the cards in order to win the game."

This book provides a few more cards — play them well!

"So much of what we call management consists of making it difficult for people to work."
~Peter Drucker

INDEX

APPENDICES

TWO COMMON REASONS WHY BUSINESSES FAIL:

FORGET THE IMPORTANCE OF PROFIT
DO NOT ACCEPT PERSONAL ACCOUNTABILITY

PERSONAL

LACK OF PERSONAL ACCOUNTABILITY:
A KEY REASON BUSINESSES FAIL

WHAT WE HEAR
WE WORK TO LIVE, NOT LIVE TO WORK
IT'S JUST A JOB
GET A LIFE
KEEP WORK SEPARATE
STAY DETACHED
IT'S NOT PERSONAL, IT'S BUSINESS

This is fine for the vast majority of the working population

**In my view however, if you are the top Exec / GM
of a business, it is
A TOTALLY PERSONAL EXPERIENCE**

How you do your job could affect the personal experiences of thousands of people. Not only your team members, but also their loved ones, dependents, etc.

This is an overwhelming sense of personal responsibility that I would wake up with every day.

I can guarantee with almost 100% certainty that when you are talking to anyone on your team about anything important, especially change, just one thought is going through their heads.

How does this affect me personally?

DEFINITIONS

ORGANIZATION
A collection of people and
assets that pursue a
common purpose

BUSINESS
An organization that has the
principle objective
of making a profit

ENTREPRENEUR
A person who
identifies
an opportunity
for
a business
to make
a profit

**BUSINESS MAN
OR WOMAN**
A person
responsible
for managing a
business

MANAGER
A person
responsible for ensuring
that the organization is
performing to its agreed
objectives in the
most cost-
effective
way

A manager is responsible for the application and performance of knowledge.

Efficiency is doing things right.   *Effectiveness is doing the right things.*

Management is doing things right.   *Leadership is doing the right things.*

~Peter Drucker

         A DAY WITH A CEO

BUSINESS BASICS   PYRAMID OF SUCCESS

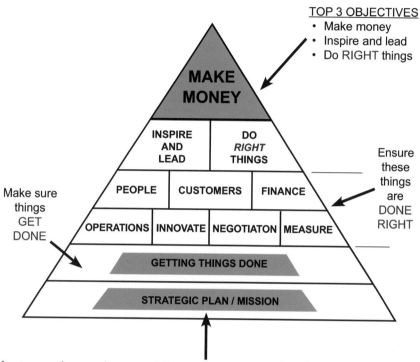

TOP 3 OBJECTIVES
- Make money
- Inspire and lead
- Do RIGHT things

MAKE MONEY

INSPIRE AND LEAD | DO *RIGHT* THINGS

PEOPLE | CUSTOMERS | FINANCE

OPERATIONS | INNOVATE | NEGOTIATON | MEASURE

GETTING THINGS DONE

STRATEGIC PLAN / MISSION

Make sure things GET DONE

Ensure these things are DONE RIGHT

All businesses have to have a guiding entrepreneurial idea that will hopefully make it money. This idea can be expressed in a few different formats.

Mission Statement / Strategic Intent / Business Plan

The success of any business will ultimately depend on if this idea is able to create wealth.

The number one objective of the GM is to understand and believe in this idea and its capability to make money.

The GM will be required to understand and "SIGN IN" to the main strategic intent of the business.

Keep this model in your head at all times.

BUSINESS BASICS

IMPORTANT ROLES OF A GENERAL MANAGER

A unique and personal role

CREATE AND MANAGE TEAMS

CREATE AND SUSTAIN CULTURE

INFLUENCE THINKING

APPOINT / CHANGE KEY EXECUTIVES

DEVELOP AND LOOK AFTER YOURSELF

FINALLY

MOST GMs WILL TELL YOU THAT THEY SPEND MOST
OF THEIR TIME ON PEOPLE AND PROBLEMS

     A DAY WITH A CEO

PEOPLE / MOTIVATION / LEADERSHIP

> "I've learned that people will forget what you said, people will forget what you did, but people will never forget how you made them feel."
> ~Maya Angelo

FAILURE TO DEVELOP PEOPLE:
A KEY REASON WHY BUSINESSES FAIL

KEY POINTS

SOMETIMES THERE ARE NO CLEAR ANSWERS

HUMAN BEHAVIOR, LARGELY, HAS TO BE EXPERIENCED, NOT TAUGHT

EVERYONE NEEDS TO BE MANAGED DIFFERENTLY

BEHAVIOR IS MORE IMPORTANT THAN WORDS

THE 15% / 70% / 15% RULE

TOP 15% PERFORMERS GUIDE, KEEP OUT OF WAY

THE MIDDLE 70%, THE AREA OF FOCUS TO IMPROVE

BOTTOM 15%, SEEK TO CORRECT OR REMOVE

BE ON GOOD TERMS WITH EVERYONE

MOTIVATION

FOUNDING FATHERS OF MOTIVATIONAL THEORY

MACHIAVELLI	1469
HAWTHORNE	1930
CARNEGIE	1930
HERZBERG	1930
MASLOW	1943

These are the main authors of Motivational Theory.
Many of today's books can be related to the thinking of the above.
Notice the dates and how they still have a lot of relevance today.
BECAUSE
Human behavior has to be experienced, not taught.
This is a lengthy process.

MACHIAVELLI

GOOD NEWS	TIMED RELEASE TO SUSTAIN MOTIVATION
BAD NEWS	ALL AT ONCE TO AVOID INSECURITY

DALE CARNEGIE

HOW TO WIN FRIENDS AND INFLUENCE PEOPLE

FAVORITE SOUND?

FAVORITE SUBJECT?

This works, so use it. Even when you know it is being used, it works!

HAWTHORNE EXPERIMENTS 1930

IF YOU TREAT PEOPLE SPECIALLY.

THEY WILL PERFORM SPECIALLY.

EVEN AGAINST LOGICAL EXPECTATION.

 A DAY WITH A CEO

> If you are not happy, it does not mean that you are unhappy, just that you are not happy.

HERZBERG

MIDDLE STATE

HYGIENE FACTORS	TRUE MOTIVATORS
Policy	Achievement
Pay	Recognition
Work Conditions	Responsibility
Status	Advancement
Personal Life	

MASLOW

HIERARCHY OF NEEDS

SELF ACTUALIZATION

ESTEEM

LOVE / BELONGING

SAFETY

PHYSIOLOGICAL

The challenge for managers is to assess where the team members are on the Hierarchy of Needs.

We all move up and down depending upon many factors. This should be looked at from a two dimensional aspect, the individual has aspirations to move up the ladder and at the same time, the job of the manager is to task the individual so that the levels are moving up to stretch and challenge! Avoiding the danger of team members finding the job too easy and reaching the SELF ACTUALIZATION level, which could be counter productive.

LEADERSHIP v. MANAGEMENT

LEADER

Focuses more on vision, direction and inspiration.

Collaborates / Persuades

Relationships

Inspires

Gains respect / Commitment

Facilitates on problem solving

Goals driven by desire

Self evaluates

HIGH EMOTIONAL INTELLIGENCE

MANAGER

Focuses more on task, execution and getting things done.

There are of course good and bad managers, and all good managers have strong leadership qualities that enable them to be effective. Pure management can however lead to some extreme behavior, which has to be guarded against, including:

Tries to control

Orders others, dictates

Instills fears

Uses positional power

Solves problems

Driven by personal need

RELIES ON IQ & INTELLIGENCE

GENERAL MANAGER

Part Leader, part Manager. A question of balance.
Where do you line up?

LEADERSHIP SKILLS CAN BE GAINED — WORK ON THEM

"Anyone wanting to be a leader among you must first be a servant. If you choose to lead you must first serve."
~World's greatest leader???

"When the best leader's work is done, the people say we did it ourselves."
~Lao-tzu

BUILDING A TEAM

LEADERSHIP IS NOT MANAGEMENT

OBJECTIVE

The purpose of creating a TEAM is because the collective output of a group of well organized, highly motivated people is greater than that of a series of individuals doing their own thing. Usually!

BENEFITS OF A TEAM

Enables a multi-skilled / multi-talented group to be formed.
Team members provide each other with back up and support.
Groups usually think more effectively than individuals.
Team spirit can produce "Heroic Results."
More members produce back up and risk resilience.

TEAM STRUCTURE

Mix different skills and styles. Finishers, Starters, Creators, Detailers, Front people, Back room folks.
Objective is effective working together.
Use some of the tools available to assess various members skill sets.

I am the master of all I see?
I have a plan!
Follow me?

"Leaders Do Not Create Followers. They Create Other Leaders."
~Tom Peters

RECRUITMENT

An expensive and time consuming process with risk.
Is it really required? Have you exhausted all internal options?
PROBABILITY OF SUCCESS CIRCA 60%

SAYING THE RIGHT THINGS
WINS THE JOB

DOING THE RIGHT THINGS
KEEPS THE JOB

RECRUITING GOOD PEOPLE

Make your business attractive

Become personally involved

Start by persuading them to work for you

Ask team members to help

Keep a database of prospects you have met

Look at process through the eyes of prospect

Close deal quickly

CHANGING JOBS

Whenever changing any job, sit down and write out two lists.

One listing the reasons why you have been successful and earned the move.

Another list outlining what you have to do to be successful in the new job.

They are nearly always different.

~Peter Drucker

 A DAY WITH A CEO

THE LEADER'S CHALLENGE

Review everyone on an individual basis

Do they have a clear brief of what is expected of them?

Do they have clear goals set with measures and incentives to achieve?

Are their hygiene factors OK? Are they unhappy about anything?

Where are they on the Maslow hierarchy?
Is the job too much, too little?

Increase or decrease load, as required.

Do they have the right training to do the job?

Do they have a contract that reflects their role and importance?

Do they have a regular review and opportunity
to discuss performance?

Have you given them a vision of where they could
develop to if successful?

Can they do more, have you asked them?

Are they stressed? Have you asked them? Have you checked?

How is their team performing?

Make them feel special and unique.

Are they passing down and spreading these points to others?

PEOPLE

CHANGE

*There is nothing more difficult to plan, more
doubtful of success, nor more difficult to manage
than the creation of a new order of things.*

~Nicholas Machiavelli

> **What is the difference between
> a man and a dog?
> If you feed a dog, it does not bite your hand.**
>
> *~Chinese Proverb*

**CHANGE is always difficult for most people to handle.
Be prepared to see some good examples of SELF INTEREST and GREED.
You can depend upon it!**

 A DAY WITH A CEO

FINANCE

MAIN SECTIONS

Basic Financial Schematic **How A Business Works**	**Accounting** **Main Reports** **P&L / Cash / Balance Sheet**
Break Even Charts **Relevance & Use**	**Absorption Costing**

MAIN ROLE OF FINANCE

To keep a numerate record of business activity (score keepers).

To provide a set of accounts for the authorities to check. Mainly for taxation purposes.

To provide forecasting guidance and direction from a numerate perspective.

To evaluate the financial impact of business decisions.

To ensure that the business is financially prudent and fiscally responsible.

To manage and support the audit of the business.

To provide financial / analytical support to the company strategy.

To ensure that all financial reporting is accurate and consistent.

Remember that the Finance Function does not run the business,
it can sometimes seem that way because they have access
to information, which is a KEY power base.

BASIC FINANCIAL SCHEMATIC

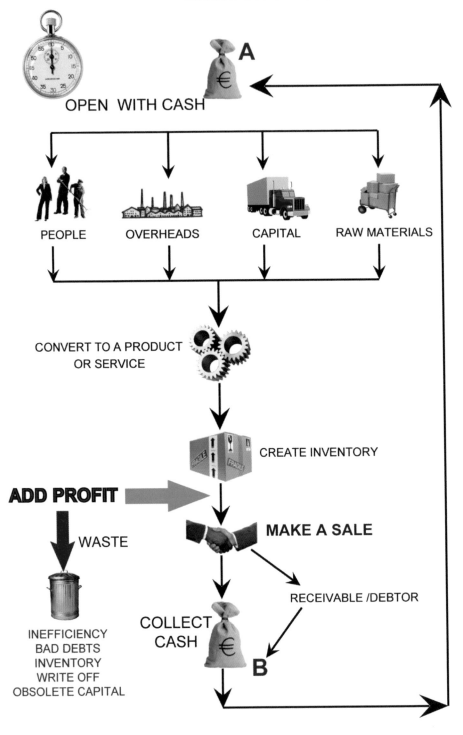

OPEN WITH CASH — **A**

PEOPLE   OVERHEADS   CAPITAL   RAW MATERIALS

CONVERT TO A PRODUCT OR SERVICE

CREATE INVENTORY

ADD PROFIT

WASTE

MAKE A SALE

RECEIVABLE /DEBTOR

COLLECT CASH — **B**

INEFFICIENCY
BAD DEBTS
INVENTORY
WRITE OFF
OBSOLETE CAPITAL

COPYRIGHT BRIAN MOORE   A DAY WITH A CEO

RULES OF FINANCE

Related to Schematic

DO NOT RUN OUT OF CASH

GO FROM A TO B AS FAST AS POSSIBLE

ADD AS MUCH PROFIT AS MARKET WILL STAND

OPERATE AS EFFICIENTLY AS POSSIBLE

REDUCE WASTE

DO NOT TIE CASH UP IN LARGE ASSETS / INVENTORY

MAXIMIZE CREDITORS (Source finance do not over do it!)

MINIMIZE DEBTORS (Collect CASH quickly)

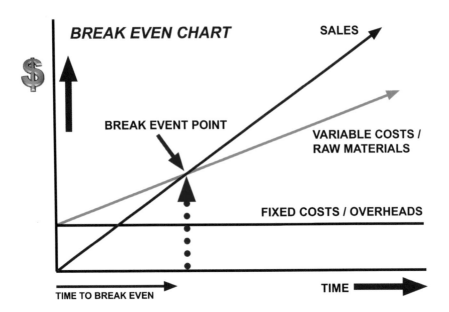

NOTES ON BREAK EVEN CHARTS

All companies have different charts and require different management.

The relationship between fixed and variable costs requires to be understood for your business.

The difference between fixed and variable costs is a function of time. In the long term all costs could be viewed as variable?

EXAMPLES OF TWO DIFFERENT COMPANIES

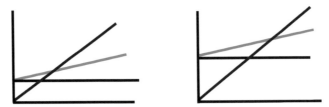

What would the various types of businesses be?

What would the management challenges be for each?

FINANCE BASIC REPORTS

PROFIT & LOSS ACCOUNT
A report covering a period of time that includes all the costs, income and expenditure of the business and any other costs as related to that time period. The difference between the income and the costs being the PROFIT.

CASH FLOW REPORT
A report covering a period of time that only shows the movements of CASH in and out of the business with the opening and starting point being the CASH IN HAND (or Not!). This is the most important report to determine business viability and capability to trade.

NO CASH = NO BUSINESS
The relationship between P&L account requires to be understood as it is more than possible for a business to be showing a healthy profit but FAIL.

BALANCE SHEET
A snapshot of the business at any moment in time. Usually at the start and end of the periods that the P&L and CASH FLOW accounts are related to. It lists all the assets and liabilities of the business and reconciles them so that they BALANCE.

ABSORPTION COSTING
The purpose of absorption costing is to allocate all business costs into one simple rate, which should make estimating and costing easier to use.
Usually a labor or machine hourly rate.

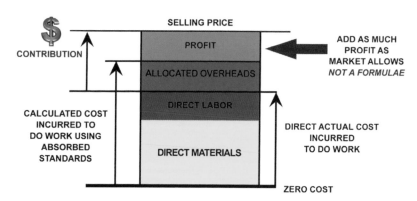

THE ISSUES WITH ABSORPTION COSTING ARE:
Volumes / hours move and can cause accounting issues.
Can mask an opportunity if contribution analysis not used.
The widespread use of marginal costing can be dangerous.

CUSTOMERS / SELLING / NEGOTIATIONS

CUSTOMERS

CASH

NO CASH   **NO BUSINESS**

SO PRETTY IMPORTANT

MAKE SURE YOU GIVE THEM WHAT THEY WANT

(Not what you think they want)

Collect the CASH

THREE MAIN ACTIVITIES WITH CUSTOMERS

IDEALLY IN THIS ORDER

LISTEN
Market Research
Market Surveys
Telephone Surveys
Sales Feedback
Complaints Department
Media

These three processes all interact

SPEAK TO
Advertising
Websites
Sales Force
Media
Mail Shots

PROVIDE GOODS AND / OR SERVICES
Good Quality
When Required
Right Price

CUSTOMERS

Fundamentally important and the whole organization culture
should be customer focused.

The GM is the number one sales person. Understand what that means.

Customers require to be managed. They are not always right!

> Good customers should be looked after and developed.
> Bad customers should be removed, or priced to acceptability.

Listening to CUSTOMERS is more important than speaking to them.

HONESTY! A more powerful weapon than you think!
Specially when you have screwed up and coming from the top Exec.
Many good things can come from open dialogue in difficult situations.

Customers are a major source of information. Use it.
Go and listen. Market / your performance / competition / opportunities.

Customers take risks dealing with you. (Buyers Risk!!)
Make sure you understand it and factor it into the pricing.

Customers expect a lot without paying for it.
Make a list of the free items you provide and decide if to charge or not.

MARKETING

Half of it is a waste of money (at least)
Unfortunately difficult to know which half.

This is talking to customers and potential customers.

Make sure objectives / cost / audience
well thought out.

Marketing people can get carried away with the power of their tools and do not
always focus on objectives and the cost of meeting them.

All products have a life cycle.
Understand what it is for yours.

SELLING

It's a basic life skill, we do it all the time.

LIFE SKILL

Listening is more important than speaking.

Customers are the ultimate judge of effectiveness.

Success and failure is clear, order or not!

COMPETITIVE

Most sales people fail most of the time!
It is a very rare sales person that converts more than 50% of the leads.

The rule of numbers usually applies.
The more prospects you deal with the more orders you get.

PROCESS    INTERPERSONAL

EVERY BUSINESS HAS ITS OWN UNIQUE SALES PIPELINE
UNDERSTAND WHAT IT IS
ALLOCATE RESOURCE TO MAXIMIZE ORDERS

PROCESS STAGES

ADDRESSABLE MARKET	AVAILABLE MARKET	SUSPECTS	PROSPECTS	QUOTES	ORDER

Determine the % conversion rate from each stage.
Particularly the expensive stages like quote preparation.
The conversion rates from quotes to orders is important.
Analyze the reasons orders lost.
How cost effectiveness is this process.

UP SELLING

You should know what all of these terms mean

BUYER'S RISK

USP

GRADING

BUNDLING

BODY LANGUAGE

BUYING SIGNAL

PRICE POINT

PRICE

SWITCH SELL

COST

CLOSING

NEGOTIATING

FABs

PARETO

DEALING WITH POOR CUSTOMERS

A REAL LIFE EXAMPLE

Pay attention. This page can make you a lot of money.

One way is to list customers into 4 groups:

Good

Could Be Good

Acceptable

X — A Nuisance

A business had 10 X customers that only contributed approximately 5% profit. The sales manager was told to DOUBLE THE PRICES for these customers.

A month later, doubling the prices was not done. Sales folks normally do not like this sort of work.

Two months later, it was still not done.

So the question is WHY? Answer — we will lose the customers.

OK, so how many will you lose? Answer — It could be at least half of them.

Out comes the calculator... Let's assume we lose 6 of the 10. OK?

The sales guy said OK, but he did not expect it to be 6.

Did following sum.

Current profit from 10 customers at 5% on say sales per customer of 100 ($ or ?) equals 50 (5% on 1,000).

Double price for 4 remaining customers profit is 105 per customer equals 420.

Outcome Profit goes from 50 to 420 on sales of 800 (4 x 200 new price) as against profit of 50 on sales of 1,000 from 10 customers.

NET RESULT
SALES FALL FROM 1,000 TO 800
PROFIT INCREASES FROM 50 TO 420

HAVE DONE THIS SO MANY TIMES AND IT WORKS
BUT ONLY IN THE MARGINS ON A SMALL NUMBER
OF X CUSTOMERS

 A DAY WITH A CEO

THINGS TO LOOK OUT FOR

This page can make you a lot of money or save you a lot of money.
Full of surprises when you ask!

Make sure the sales negotiators are financially numerate

Some questions to ask

- If you mark the cost of a product up by 10% then give the customer a 10% discount what is the % profit?

- If you mark the cost of a product up by 50%, what is the % Gross Margin?

- If the company bottom line profit is 10% of total sales revenue:

  What will the new profit % be if you give a 5% discount across the board?

  What will the percentage increase in profit be if you increase all prices by 1%?

- If you have a business with a large number of products with a price list, go through the list and selectively price taking a lesson from the grocery business.

  Use price points. Price the most noticeable items competitively. Load less visible items.

- Do an exercise with the sales team. List all of the things you do for customers FREE. See if any of these can be charged for.

Great area for instant 100% profit and cash.

Make sure the SALES TEAM understands the following terms for your business / products / contracts.

PROFIT / GROSS MARGIN / CONTRIBUTION / MARK UP / ABSORBED COST / DIRECT COST

MORE CAN BE LESS

Most businesses chase and maximize sales.
Sometimes taking out the few worst performing lowest margin customers can increase profitability and make the business much more effective.
Less work more profit.

WHAT IS NEGOTIATING?
THE PROCESS OF TRYING TO CHANGE SOMEONE'S MIND

THE PROCESS

PREPARATION.....PRE-SELLING / CONDITIONING

EXPLORATION.....FACE-TO-FACE

OBJECTIVE CLARIFICATION.....IN THEIR MIND

FIRST DEMAND.....IDEALLY FROM THEM

COUNTER PROPOSAL.....NON-POSITIONAL BARGAINING

EXCHANGE.....CONCESSIONS.....PRESSURE

CLOSURE

 A DAY WITH A CEO

KEY POINTS OF NEGOTIATING

IT IS A FUNDAMENTAL LIFE SKILL

IT IS A PROCESS NOT AN EVENT

IT STARTS EARLY ON

IT REQUIRES CONSTANT ATTENTION AND UPDATING

STAY OBJECTIVE. DO NOT FALL IN LOVE A WITH DEAL

DECIDE WALK AWAY POSITION UP FRONT. STICK TO IT

OUTCOMES NORMALLY FOLLOW ECONOMICAL REALITY

IT IS ABOUT HAVING A VETO

FOCUS ON THE BOTTOM LINE

MAKE SURE THE CASH FLOW WORKS
ESPECIALLY ON FOREIGN TRANSACTIONS

CRITICAL SUCCESS FACTORS

INVEST HEAVILY IN PLANNING.
I know what I must get, should get and could get.

NEVER CONCEDE FOR GOODWILL.
Tie strings to all concessions.

HAVE A STRONG OPENING BID.
Aim as high as credibly possible.

ADOPT CONDITIONAL BARGAINING.
If you....., Then I.....

NEGOTIATING TIPS

NEGOTIATING IS A PROCESS
BE PREPARED AND HAVE A PLAN

Strategize outcomes and
work out who does what
What information you need
Roll play outcomes

TEAM WORK ALL IMPORTANT

No prima donnas please

UNDERSTAND THE PROCESS

**Time Table / Sequence of Events /
Decision Criteria / Sealed Bids / How
Many Chances To Submit / When
Decision Made and Who By**

LISTEN   LEARN   ACT   (ESPECIALLY LISTEN)

BE PATIENT

DO NOT PLAY GAMES. THEY ARE OVER RATED

FIND OUT WHO YOU ARE DEALING WITH
Are you talking to the deal maker / approver? If not, who is it? Is the opportunity real? It may just be a research exercise.

DO NOT RELY ON PULLING RABBITS
OUT OF THE HAT

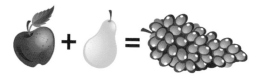 BE PREPARED TO TRADE

UNDERSTAND AND WATCH
BODY LANGUAGE

 DO NOT GET STRANDED

CLOSE THE DEAL

PRICING DO NOTs

- Mention price too early
- Give discounts
- Use marginal costing / pricing
- Focus on price. Sell FABS & USPS
- Provide analysis opportunities

PRICING DOs

- Analyze all supplies and costs
- Understand competition
- Assess buyers risk
- Identify benefits
- Bundle where possible
- Do not give away early
- Concessions... Seek trade...Time limit
- Avoid wars
- Identify non-discretionary areas
- Charge what the customer will pay

QUESTION

YOUR PRICES ARE JUST FAR TOO HIGH!

ANSWER

COMPARED TO WHAT?

OPERATIONS / MANAGEMENT / PLANNING

OPERATIONS

OPERATIONS IS DEFINED AS THE PRODUCTION OR PROCUREMENT OF THE PRODUCTS OR SERVICES THAT THE BUSINESS SELLS

This is a huge subject and operations probably consumes most of the costs incurred in the business.

This book does not cover all the various operational issues and opportunities.

From a general management perspective you will require to determine how your operations are being managed and use the data and questions in this book to evaluate performance.

HOWEVER SOME KEY STRATEGIC QUESTIONS REQUIRE TO BE ADDRESSED

Make v. buy....What do you want to make v. buy in?

Supply chain. Where do you fit in and what are the implications?

Raw material supply — how secure / volatile?

Low cost /off shore manufacturing strategy?

What is the continuous improvement culture / plan?

MEASUREMENT & CONTROLS

If it can not be measured, it can not be managed!

WHY MEASURE?
Provide information
Communication aide
Track specific activities
Identify correct problems early
Determine and justify decisions
Planning aide
Risk management aide

> **"In the land of the blind, the one-eyed man is king."**
> *~Erasmus*

WHY HAVE CONTROLS

AN OPPORTUNITY TO HELP
This provides the senior Executive to take an overview of a situation and see if any help can be provided.

TO INFORM
It provides the information to let Executives know what is going on.

TO POLICE
Make sure company assets are prudently managed and deployed.

KEY POINT
When a control is introduced, Executives often think they are a waste of time as they end up approving everything they see.
The point with a control is that the effectiveness is often invisible as the higher the level of authority, it acts as a deterrent to stop frivolous / marginal requests being presented. Stopped at the source!

You are controlling what you do not see!

 A DAY WITH A CEO

INFORMATION

ESSENTIAL

Information is essential to enable Executives to make decisions and to control events.

POWERFUL

Information is a key lever of power.

EXPENSIVE

Costs money to produce, circulate, read and store. Can waste a lot of time producing.

MAKE SURE REALLY REQUIRED BEFORE REQUESTING

COMMUNICATION TOOL

The nearer you are to the event, the less you need information.

The further away, the more communication it gives you.

CAN BE MISLEADING

If it is important it should be cross-checked; sources validated.

CAN BE MISUSED

People can be very selective just to get something done their way.

CAN BE IMPERFECT

Execs constantly have to make decisions using less than perfect information.

It is either not available, not timely or just too expensive to find.

A key skill of the GM is to make JUDGEMENTS / DECISIONS on less than perfect data.

WHY ASK FOR INFORMATION?

Not only because you want to know, but also because you think the provider should know.

Always ask the sender if they are only giving you the information because they think only for YOU? Especially with regular reports that may have used up their shelf life?

IT CAN IMPROVE PERFORMANCE BY JUST BEING PRESENT

Doing nothing can be risky

There is nothing more difficult to plan, more doubtful of success, nor more difficult to manage than the creation of new order of things.

~Nicholas Machiavelli, 1469

A BUSINESS PLAN HAS TO HAVE NUMBERS IN IT
Definition of a business report is numbers joined by words.

PLAN DETAIL WITHIN THE HORIZON OF THE BUSINESS ABILITY TO CHANGE

MOST PLANS FAIL. HAVE A CONTINGENCY / RISK SECTION

MAKE IT CLEAR WHO HAS TO DO WHAT AND BY WHEN

"Failures in two 2 classes.
Those who thought, but never did.
Those that did, but never thought."
~John Charles Salak

PLANNING

INNOVATION

An idea is
good until disproven.
An assumption is bad until
validated.

"Good ideas often
come from the wrong people
at the wrong time for the
wrong reasons."
~Tom Peters

INNOVATE OR DIE
KEY POINTS

GROWTH THE GOD

Virtually all the economies of the world rely on growth, which is ultimately fed by population growth. This is ongoing and potentially scary (approaching 7BN). Not wishing to debate if growth is good or bad, and there are arguments, the reality is that most Execs in most businesses are expected to grow the business.

ORGANIC GROWTH

This the natural growth in a company that arises from serving a growing market. As against taking market share or introducing new innovative products and services. Enjoy it if it is good, but remember that nothing is forever so have plans to deal with any market down turn or slowing of growth.

INNOVATION

Organic growth may not always sustain the growth aspirations of a business so other innovations have to be introduced to achieve growth. These would include:

INTERNAL INNOVATION	EXTERNAL INNOVATION
CONTINUOUS IMPROVEMENT	ACQUISITIONS
R & D	JOINT VENTURES
NEW PRODUCT DEVELOPMENT	LICENSING TECHNOLOGY
NEW CUSTOMERS	COMMISSION NEW PRODUCTS

 A DAY WITH A CEO

PRODUCT DEVELOPMENT REVIEW

ROUTE 1 — The easiest?

If you have good customer relationships and have established commercial trading arrangements, then these customers should be the most amenable to try any new products. Especially if they have been involved in their development.

ROUTE 2 — Maybe easy

This will require the establishment of new customers and maybe new markets success will depend upon the quality and market ability of the product.

ROUTE 3 — Probably the hardest to do

This will require you to develop the new product and find new customers maybe in a different market where not known? Success will depend upon the quality of the product or more probably the BRAND image of the company.

NOTE

Most companies are doing 1 and 2 all the time as a natural extension of their business evolution.

Activity 3 tends to imply a more revolutionary approach to new products and market development.

A DAY WITH A CEO

GETTING THINGS DONE

**THIS SECTION IS ABOUT THE ACTION COMPONENT OF
MANAGEMENT FROM A PRACTICAL PERSPECTIVE**

CONTENTS

*No problem
can withstand the assault of
sustained thinking.*

~Voltaire

DEFINE TASK / HAVE A PLAN

BRAIN PATH / MIND MAP

A creative technique that is helpful

The above is an example of a Brain Path, which is a process that can be a very effective creative thinking tool.

 A DAY WITH A CEO

UNDERSTAND YOURSELF
BUSINESS LEADERS VALUE SYSTEM
(Operating System most of us are programmed for)

THE FAITH
As an observer of management behaviour, it is clear that we all act with certain beliefs . . . some notable ones for thought.

COMMON SENSE IS COMMON
Unfortunately NOT!

TELEPATHY EXISTS
A common discussion heard in most teams –

> **Team Member to Leader:** *"I have just about had it with so and so, they have let me down again."*
> **Leader:** *"Have you told them what you expect?"*
> **Team Member:** *"Hell no, they should know that!"*

Assume nothing, especially if the outcome of any action is critically important. Ask the obvious, the answers are often surprising!

PLANS WORK
I am still waiting!

An essential business tool as a reference framework, which has to have a risk analysis correlated to the cost and implication of failure.

STRANGERS ARE WONDERFUL
When we are dissatisfied with the performance of a team member, we often assume that we can hire someone we never met who probably knows nothing about our business and may not even exist. Touching really – probability of success 50 – 60% if you have a 'good' recruitment process.

> *Hiring is a powerful tool, but keep the probability of success in perspective.*

PEOPLE LISTEN
Yes, right, sure. Probably the most underrated management skill that receives virtually no training – the ability to LISTEN. Listening is not just NOT SPEAKING!

TIME IS INFINITE
We often just carry on assuming we have all the time in the world to do anything.

I RUN THIS WELL SO I CAN RUN THAT WELL
A basic belief of managers is that success is always directly due to their own personal ability and therefore can be replicated. This requires other factors— Market, Business Culture, Luck, Events. Many times success is a one hit wonder. Right time, right place.

*You may not agree, but **the evidence is overwhelming!***

POWER

Power is a key requirement in any action plan.

Where the POWER rests requires to be understood and also the way that POWER changes in a dynamic situation (like a negotiation).

FORMS OF POWER

POSITIONAL

INFORMATION

WEALTH

KNOWLEDGE AND RESPECT

PHYSICAL

ACTION REQUIRES POWER

INTENT CAN BE STOPPED BY POWER

YOU NEED TO DETERMINE WHERE THE POSITIVE AND NEGATIVE POWER IS IN ANY IMPORTANT ACTIVITY OF CHANGE

DO THIS AS A FORMAL ASSESSMENT

ALWAYS FOLLOW THE CASH ESPECIALLY IN A DISPUTE

WHO HAS THE CASH IN HAND?

KNOW YOUR BUSINESS

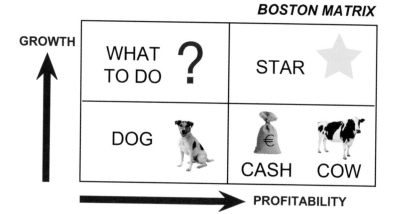

BOSTON MATRIX

DETERMINE WHERE YOU BUSINESS FITS INTO
THE MATRIX AND THEN FORM A STRATEGY/PLAN
FOR WHERE YOU WOULD LIKE IT TO BE.

GO HUNTING

*All businesses create areas of waste and
inefficiency that creeps in over time.*

Frequently the Managers close to the situation are unaware of cost creep and may
be complacent.

The GM has a responsibility to challenge all costs to purge cost creep
and inefficiency.

For example, several Executives will order a 10% cut of head count every 5 years
as a counter measure to cost creep.

AREAS TO LOOK

Poor performers
All areas of waste look at the statistics
Information freaks creating long hours of data preparation
Politicians with not a lot to do
External service providers
Bad customers
Corporate staff

ACTION PLAN BASICS

KEY POINTS

THREE COMPONENTS:

DEFINE A PLAN OR TASK

EDUCATION / KNOWLEDGE

MOTIVATION

OR PUT MORE SIMPLY

Do you know what needs to be done, have you communicated that to the person who needs to do it and do they know how to do it and have you given them the incentive / reason to do it?

PERSONAL BALANCE SHEET

For my first real job, the boss sat me down at the beginning of every year and drew up a Balance Sheet. One side showed how much it cost the business to employ me. On the other side it showed the savings that I achieved on the various projects that I was given. A really useful way to look at your employment.

Stripping all the EGO and BS out of it, remember that you are hired as a paid employee to look after the best interests of the business, which happens to be making money!

STOP SPENDING IT

The quickest way to make money for a business is to STOP SPENDING IT!
Develop a range of activities to reduce spend the main ones being.
Work with suppliers to reduce costs.
Improve operating efficiencies across the company.
Review people costs.
Watch sales activity: Discounts / Credit notes / Give aways Marketing.

FROM CUSTOMERS

Virtually all of the income will come from customers, so the more customers and the larger the sales usually the better. So drive the sales force to increase sale (profitably of course, quality not quantity).

Pricing is the single biggest way to make an impact on PROFITABILITY. In a typical business a 1% price increase will produce a 10% PROFIT increase.

Amazing therefore that so few top people in a company are actively involved in the day-to-day pricing decisions.

POWER OF 1%

Most businesses are managed reasonably well most of the time. It is unusual for any large "low-hanging fruit" opportunities to exist. The job of Management is to work on improvements across the board to seek out often small single-digit percent savings.

The 1% Exercise is a good example, which illustrates that a 1% improvement across all the activities of a business. Specially PRICING could produce a nearly 30% improvement in profitability.

VOLTAIRE QUOTES (1694 -1778)

"Each player must accept the cards life deals him or her: but once they are in hand, he or she alone must decide how to play the cards in order to win the game."

"Every man is guilty of all the good he didn't do."

"Illusion is the first of the pleasures."

"I disapprove of what you say, but I will defend to the death your right to say it."

"Work saves us from three great evils: boredom, vice and need."

"Think for yourselves and let others enjoy the privilege to do so too."

"Doubt is not a pleasant condition, but certainty is absurd."

"Judge of a man by his questions rather than by his answers."

"Prejudice is opinion without judgement."

"A witty saying proves nothing."

"All the reasonings of men are not worth one sentiment of women."

"Appreciation is a wonderful thing: It makes what is excellent in others belong to us as well."

"Behind every successful man stands a surprised mother-in-law."

"Business is the salt of life."

"Common sense is not so common."

"No problem can withstand the assault of sustained thinking."

         A DAY WITH A CEO

OBSERVATIONS ON LIFE

PEOPLE POWER

This book addresses the most important aspect of management, which is that "PEOPLE MAKE THINGS HAPPEN." Consequently, leadership is a key art of management.

SMELL THE DAISIES

Experience shows that some and often many of the activities managers run around doing do not actually move the business forward.

The "indispensable Me!" trap is easy to fall into.

Take time out for leisure and exercise – It recharges the energy and most importantly time away from the business is often a rich source of creative thought.

KEEP SMILING

Humour is a powerful tool and has advantages:

> *Health*
> *Stress relieving*
> *Maintaining perspective*
> *Bonding*

> *An open, friendly good-humoured team will usually perform well and it will be more fun!*

COMMON SENSE NOT THAT COMMON

Experience has taught me that what is obvious to me is not to others and common sense is far from common.

ONE, TWO, THREE RULE!

The first time something goes wrong it is probably bad luck.

The second time it goes wrong it may be you?

*The third time it goes wrong, **IT IS YOU!***

LIFE'S NOT FAIR

When I started in business I had an idealistic view of life. I believed in politicians and that policemen were fair and honest, etc. I always believed that the good guys prospered and that ability and hard work had its just rewards.

Now I realise that good guys can get shot! And that crooks do sometimes win!

Be realistic with people's motives.

ACTIONS NOT WORDS

What people do is more important than what they say. Most people can form the words of intent that impress. Few deliver the goods! So:

Do as you say and say as you do!
Watch behaviour, this is more important words.

RELATIONSHIPS v. ECONOMIC REALITY

I am a big fan of relationships; they are usually fundamental to success and make the world go round. However, a word of warning! Most business performance decisions usually default to "Economic Reality."

Few relationships survive a 10% discount.
~Peter Drucker

Managing

By

Walking

About

Very effective

COMMUNICATING

WHAT IS YOUR HORSE'S NAME?

On vacation in the Greek islands I decided to provide a little insight into how to get on with people to my three young children.

So, we approached a line of locals who were giving horse and cart rides. I pick out the most miserable driver with the most decrepit horse. This man just did not want to be doing this job.

So, we all pile into the carriage and with a grunt the driver starts.

After a short while I start the lesson.

"So, what's your name?" I ask.
Signs of life and some communication.
"And what's your horse's name?"

Animated response and the driver's whole attitude changed. The lesson from dad was a raving success.

Unfortunately, for several years after that whenever the family all jumped into a cab and I asked the driver what his name was, it was followed quickly by a chorus of:

"And what's your horse's name?"

It can sometimes be a cross helping people to understand!

DON'T LEAVE ME BEHIND

An important part of leadership is to create the vision of where the team is going and to constantly invent and recycle initiatives to keep motivating.

This usually means that the leader's brain process may have opened up a gap between strategic intent and the ability of the team to act / implement. Make sure this 'gap' is managed or else the team become confused and nothing is completed – confusion reigns!

**HEARING, LISTENING,
UNDERSTANDING
— Not the same**

GOOD QUESTIONS

One of the little things I do with up-and-coming leaders is to ask them to do a little exercise often to their obvious irritation.

The task is to ask the next person they are in communication with two questions, after they have had a conversation/briefing:

What have I just told you?

What are you now going away to do?

The result is usually a seriously depressed person who had believed that they were excellent communicators.

They had been paying more attention to the transmit mode and not enough to the receive mode.

LANGUAGE

We all realise that if an English speaking person needs to talk with a Chinese speaking person then there are some obvious clues that interpretation skills may be required and care has to be taken when communicating.

However, communication dangers can often be right under our very noses where we least expect them even within the same language group.

MUST BE TRUE – READ IT IN THE MINUTES

The written record of an event (Report, Minutes) takes on a considerable importance, particularly in a dispute situation and/or where larger companies are involved. Make sure that the written word reflects your intent. Try to secure control of the minute writing at meetings, pay attention to checking drafts. Carelessness and lack of attention could come back to haunt you.

**AN IDEA IS GOOD UNTIL
DISPROVEN
AN ASSUMPTION IS BAD
UNTIL VALIDATED**

THINGS YOU SHOULD KNOW

SILENCE IS GOLDEN

*A most powerful and badly used tool – most managers like the sound of their own voice far too much. Let the silence create answers from people you are talking to, especially when negotiating. It can be unnerving but sometimes **mouth shut and waiting** is the best option.*

This is often a good strategy with a difficult negotiation when you have laid out the situation and the other person has to respond – so you shut up and wait – and wait! Make sure your team understand the power of silence – I have unfortunately witnessed situations where a position has been outlined and as the silence starts, a team member takes the opportunity to dive in to reiterate your point – letting the other side off the hook.

You usually do not learn with your mouth working.

LET'S GET OUT OF HERE

Business leadership is basically about getting results. Make sure the objectives are clearly defined and once achieved – move on.

Best example is the "salesman who gets the order," but then feels it necessary to carry on talking about the decision process. This activity is high risk as the only possible outcome is a cancelled order. Get out. Move on to the next objective (customer).

A MYSTERY

One of the points an experienced executive will make is that the presence of information produces an improved performance. So many times I have seen a Key Performance Indicator (KPI) established and by taking no further actions the performance has improved.

I am sure the industrial psychologists will have a good answer, but I believe that the answer lies in the personal belief system of individuals who instinctively always strive to improve. Leaders should focus on this pragmatic fact and introduce information often and effectively.

Clearly this is only the starting point, the next stage almost inevitably requires some more structured analytical work to achieve further improvements.

Measurements and analytical data are key to improvement. If you are unable to measure it then you usually can't improve it. However, some of the most important success criteria for the business are often very difficult to measure – e.g., morale, customer satisfaction.

THE E IN EMAILS STANDS FOR ETERNAL. THEY CAN BE DISCOVERED FROM WAY BACK AT ALL TIMES. EVEN IF DOUBLE DELETED! MAKE SURE YOU DO NOT PUT ANYTHING IN THEM THAT YOU ARE NOT PREPARED TO EXPLAIN LATER.

GO FIGURE!!

A very experienced and normally rational executive that I once worked with believed that guys who did not wear a belt were clearly not suitable for employment. A view incidentally backed up with years of his experience and with some notable examples.

Watch out for prejudices.

INTELLIGENCE CAN GET IN THE WAY

The other thing I have learned is that good leadership is not the automatic by-product of intelligence and academic excellence. Quite the reverse, the highly intelligent Executive with good qualifications often has great difficulty doing the ordinary things that create leadership – for example, walking round chatting and finding out what is going on (an activity I describe as constructively wasting time!).

DON'T FORGET THE FLOWERS

In a complex capital sale to a large UK utility, we were asked for a reference site for the customer to visit – naturally San Francisco was selected, as Manchester (UK) did not have the same appeal.

The trip cost our company £20,000 with airfares, entertainment, etc. Our Sales VP thoughtfully sent flowers to the customers' wives cost £100. We got the order and guess what they remember most!

DO YOU KNOW WHAT YOU DON'T KNOW

An interesting philosophical question that has tremendous implications for Business Leadership. We are exposed to a whole battery of information, which we have to sort out to glean what is important. It is also important that the leader checks on other (maybe inexperienced) team members to ensure that their knowledge levels are acceptable for the task in hand.

ODDS ARE AGAINST YOU

One of the active debates about leadership is "Born to or Trained."
Hopefully, this book includes loads of tips and situations that may aid leadership skills. A word of warning however, in that the items in this book will work for some people and not others, it may work for some people on one day and not another day, it may work in one circumstance and not another. So just imagine the many permutations of Personality Mood circumstance, etc.

The odds are heavily loaded against success in all circumstances.

 A DAY WITH A CEO

NOT ALL ABOUT YOU

THE FISH VAN

So, my first job as a CEO, and a small manufacturing unit has to be closed and moved to the main works. Approximately 30 long-serving team members, mainly women assembly workers, average length of service 15 years.

Being keen and wanting to communicate the exercise well, I thought through all the issues and rehearsed my announcement.

Night before, a touch nervous and lost a little sleep, the day comes and I stand up and lay out the issues and actions, to be met with that sea of blank faces (as is often the case by the way and should not discourage you from mass communications).

"Any Questions?" I ask.

"Will the fresh fish van that comes on Tuesdays be allowed to call at the main works?"

"Will we be able to play Bingo on the main works announcement system during our break time?"

The point . . .

Team members often have personal agenda items/issues that may not even be in the visibility of the leader.

**Find out what is important to the team, it may help you
achieve what is important to you.**

I FEEL BETTER FOR THAT

When communicating, especially formally and in a combative situation, avoid the temptation to "SORT PEOPLE OUT." We all do it. When launching a communication remember the basic principles. "What do I want the person who receives the communication to do after receiving it?" Therefore:

- *What should be included to ensure that the receiver is "motivated" to achieve that objective?*
- *How do I check up that the communication has achieved its objective?*

Very rarely is the answer to these questions "I feel better." "That showed him." "He thinks I'm an idiot!"

Be objective, focused and dispassionate! Not always easy.

YOU FEELING BETTER —
NOT A CREDIBLE OBJECTIVE

WHAT'S IN IT FOR ME?

Self interest, a wonderful thing and the most predictable aspects of dealing with people. In any transaction, especially if important, make sure you have worked out "what's in it for them" and "what's in it for you" if this is not readily obvious.

Worry! You have probably missed something.

Make sure your motives are objective and clearly focused!!

*What is the difference between
a man and a dog?
If you feed a dog, it does not bite your hand.
~Chinese Proverb*

Appreciate who feeds you!

DO I HAVE TO?

Unpleasant tasks are part of being a leader. It is easy to defer these tasks because of how "we feel about it," not wanting to be "the bad guy," not wanting to give people "bad news," not making the call that will give you bad news.

The disciplined leader will tackle these difficult areas quickly, effectively and professionally.

Many times when I have procrastinated about a decision then eventually get around to doing it, the overriding thought is usually "I wish I had done that earlier."

**Face up to unpleasant tasks quickly and deal with them.
Popularity is a bonus. Fairness and respect are more important.**

PICKING A FIGHT?

If you feel the need to pick a fight, company or individual, ask the following questions first:

**Do they owe me money?
What are the chances of winning?
How much will the fight cost in time and money?
Is this a fundamental integrity issues that I have to challenge?**

Look at the answers and then decide if worth going ahead.

THIS IS ABOUT YOU

THAT MOMENT You Realise

Another big lesson about leadership was learned the very first day I was appointed as Managing Director —"THAT MOMENT" you realise that you are a leader!

THE SCENE . . .

I had just been promoted to my first Managing Director position… distressed company… called a staff meeting… had a plan… gave a full brief… everyone actioned with key tasks.

The team gets up and leaves, the door shuts… you are alone.

The loneliness of leadership hits me for the first time! So what do you do?

Follow them out and ask if they understood the action plan?

Start to do one of the actions you have just delegated? You can obviously do it better than the person you just delegated it to!!

Start work on a different strategy, to really confuse everyone?

HIDE? Certainly keeping out the way has more merit than it may at first appear.

Leadership can be lonely!

Teams sometimes have to be left alone to get on with the job with minimum interference from the leader.

You may be alone with an option. A business is not a democracy. Opinions count, but not always carry vote.

GOLDFISH BOWL

Leaders are often in constant view with their actions being continually assessed. Often judged from afar!

Always watch what people do rather than what they say.

When running large teams, one to one contact may be very limited so those quick exchanges "sound bites" can be very important.

PRESSING THE BUTTON

You will not go very far in any company without being exposed to a series of tests designed to profile you by personality, suitability for the job, etc. Most are based round psychometric testing principles and can be very useful. However, in the workplace most of us at some time have to behave out of character, "Press the Button," and behave differently. If for example, we lead a team and a presentation is required and this is in our discomfort zone, you have to press the button and go for it!

CAN I REALLY DO THAT?

Talk to any team leader and they will almost certainly say that the biggest joy of the job is to see team members grow and in particular do things that they did not think possible.

Team members need to be encouraged to do things that they did not think possible.

The limitation to most activities lies between our ears.

THINK IN THREES

When milking a cow the most effective stool has three legs as it is the most stable answer for uneven surfaces.

Thinking in threes is surprisingly effective. For example: Most people only remember three points on a presentation.

Three legs of a plan is more robust than two and could survive if one activity is not working.

LESS CAN BE MORE

Avoid chasing maximum sales at all cost.

Those last incremental sales are often at very low margin.

Many businesses would benefit from a small reduction in the low margin nuisance sales/customers.

BE ON GOOD TERMS WITH ALL PERSONS

Not goodwill to mankind and peace on earth however commendable those high ideals are… An early lesson for me.

Working for a brewing company, it owned restaurants that had managers employed by the company.

Monday, a manager was caught stealing food and as a result fired! Wednesday, he was employed by an independent restaurant that happened to be one of the brewery's largest independent accounts.

Friday, he was in having lunch with the board of directors as a VIP customer.

Strange, but true…

I can think of many more examples of this nature, especially your most difficult supplier/competitor turning up as your most important customer in a key role.

Remember the ass you kick today may be the one you have to kiss tomorrow!

TIME MANAGEMENT

Like so many things, the words do not mean what you think!

If you ever believe that you can manage time let me know as soon as possible please?

It's YOU! who requires the management, not TIME!

 A DAY WITH A CEO

THINGS TO WATCH OUT FOR

LET'S GO CONQUERING

Successful teams want to grow. Spectacular growth can be achieved through acquisitions. This activity is primarily driven by management ego and professional advisors ambitions (fees).

Remember certain key facts:

    A. Success at best will be 50:50
    B. The cultural fit is critical to successful integration
    C. The bills are enormous

Fortunately, for most managers the water is so muddy after the event that the frequent bad outcomes are not obvious.

Despite the warnings, if you do get it right, the results can be spectacular.

SUPERSTARS

All teams love their best people, they seek them out train them better, promote them quicker, reward them higher. Quite right too, they can make a big difference to the team's performance. However, in most teams they are few in number unless you are very lucky. So the majority of the team do not come in for the superstar treatment. The challenge is to move the 70% performers to 80%, not the 120% people to 140%. (They will get there on their own.)

INEFFICIENCY HAS ITS REWARDS

My dear friends in the legal and financial service sector often explain how hard done by they are. I counter by explaining that we in the wealth creation business strive to achieve as much as possible at minimum (optimum) cost in as short a time as possible, whereas, in the legal/financial world reward is related to time spent, so business success is about taking as long as possible and often by working in the most inefficient way.

Just watch it when they are on your pay cheque.

EGO RATIONING

The leader should recognise that everyone has an EGO that needs feeding but that this can vary between individuals.

Do not claim all the accolades for yourself to feed your own EGO.

When all is said and done.
Usually more is said than done!!

ONLY THE CHAIRMAN'S NIECE

Salesman arrives in reception for an appointment with a top customer and finds a new receptionist, who clearly is not up-to-speed on the company and procedures or the salesman (very new car outside). Eventually the salesman blows the receptionist out the water. He meets his customer, and during the polite chitchat finds out that his favourite niece was covering reception for a couple of weeks during her college vacation – oops!!

Bit like the people who treat secretaries and PAs with no courtesy... anyone messing with an assistant can be in trouble big time... they nearly always tell afterwards!

And the point is that in a collection of human beings, relationships may exist. Formal, family, interest groups, lovers, you never know all the intricate aspects of the interpersonal relationships in a large team.

Being a bit naughty, they can sometimes be used to advantage as informal communication that hits the spot through diverse channels... dangerous, but can be fun!

I also believe you can tell a lot about a person by the way they treat people they "perceive" not to be important to them.

BULLY BOYS (and GIRLS!)

I have to admit that this is an area of internal conflict and mixed views. On the one hand I believe that aggressive unreasonable behaviour has no place in a team, but on the other hand I have seen it work well and achieve good results ... so why?

I have come to the conclusion that it is because people are far more perceptive and forgiving about aggressive verbal utterances as they are capable of filtering out what may just be superficial behaviour (getting your attention as it were) providing they have a basic respect for the leader and his/her motives.

I have seen unreasonable and aggressive behaviour work in two specific situations. Hands on distressed businesses where time is of the essence and you have little to lose, or where a visiting senior figure descends occasionally, breathes fire and leaves (usually for the regular Execs to sort out the damage, but maybe feed on the fear created).

Aggressive and unreasonable behaviour normally has no place in a well-managed team. However, it can be effective if carefully used with good intent and with the correct motivation.

BAD THINGS HAPPEN

BAD PLACES

I have had the good fortune to lead some very successful teams and some not so successful teams as judged by financial standards. The most important lesson I have learned is that the correlation between success and ability, intelligence and hard work is far from perfect. I have witnessed well-managed, highly-able teams go down in flames and a load of incompetent idiots make a fortune.

Being in the right place (market conditions?) at the right time is very important.

Bad places do however, have some interesting upsides as they are often the place where good leaders start. Even in large well-managed companies there will be some weak areas and it is often the up-and-coming leader that is given the chance to perform…working on the theory of nothing to lose and everything to gain.

Bad places consume serious time from some of our best people. Despite loads of research that proves that management time is best spent moving good situations on even further; we almost hypnotically chase lost causes.

Inexperienced leaders are often not prepared to accept defeat despite evidence that the outcome is obvious.

Failure is a part of business life. It can be debilitating, but it needs to be dealt with and put into perspective.

Good leaders will use failure for therapy. It creates a human side to the leader, creates a "permission to fail culture." This will encourage team members to try things, push the envelope as they say.

Success or failure is not necessarily due to personal performance.

Treat both appropriately and move on!

Do not waste time on lost causes.

Give me the strength to change
the things that I can.
The patience to deal with the things that I can not.
The wisdom to know the difference.

USEFUL POINTS

DEVIL'S IN THE DETAIL!

Leaders are often focussing on the "bigger picture." Sometimes it is important to ensure the detail is right. If it's really important, check every word and every grammar point.

Make sure you understand simple legal terms for example, the difference between "reasonable" and "best." Check language, such as "will" or "may."

Take the time to check it – get someone else to check your own personal work.

10 X 1 CAN BE GREATER THAN 10

Here is a tip for getting more money off customers on long and complex contracts. Keep raising a series of small invoices for extras, variations as you go and keep the amount raised for each transaction within the signing limit of the customer's junior staff.

If you wait and save all these costs up for the big extra bill at the end, it is always inevitable that senior management will negotiate a lower compromise sum – as you do!!

WHEN BEING ATTACKED

Best defence is usually to listen!

SPEAK SLOWLY

People credit you as being more knowledgeable.

PERSONAL AGENDA

In this tricky world a lot of people will be pursuing a personal agenda at the expense of the best interests of the business. Watch out for it.

CHASING LOST CAUSES

It takes a lot more energy and time to get from failure to mediocrity than from good to Excellent. Use your time wisely.

IT CAN BE ABOUT TAKING OUT LOSERS

A lesson from the Venture Capitalists

Say you make 10 investments, they would expect 2 or 3 to be very successful, the most to be average and a couple of losers. Taking out the losers quickly to save cash and time depletion is critical to success.

SLEEP

Get a good night's sleep. Tiredness affects performance and thinking.

"People need to be reminded more often than they need to be instructed."
~Samuel Johnson

 A DAY WITH A CEO

NUMBERS YOU SHOULD KNOW

TYPICAL COMPANY NUMBERS AS A % OF SALES
On a direct cash basis not absorbed rates

SPEND ON DIRECT MATERIALS	30%
COST OF EMPLOYING PEOPLE	30%
OVERHEADS NON PEOPLE COSTS	30%
PROFIT BEFORE TAX & INTEREST	10%

SOME WHAT IFs?   IMPACT ON PROFIT

UPSIDES

10% INCREASE IN SALES   **PROFIT INCREASES BY** 40%
With no overhead increase, just direct cost.

5% REDUCTION IN PEOPLE   **PROFIT INCREASES BY** 15%

5% SAVING IN MATERIAL SPEND   **PROFIT INCREASES BY** 15%

1% INCREASE IN PRICES   **PROFIT INCREASES BY** 10%

DOWNSIDES

5% INCREASE IN PAY   **PROFIT DOWN BY** 15%

5% DISCOUNT TO CUSTOMERS   **PROFIT DOWN BY** 50%

MAKE SURE YOU KNOW THE REAL NUMBERS FOR YOUR BUSINESS

AN AREA FOR CREATIVE ACCOUNTING AND DELUSION

Especially where Absorption costing is used

Do the following when determining actual savings:

FOLLOW THE CASH

- If head count is being reduced, ask for names / dates / costs.
- If inter-company transactions are involved, look at net position.
- If hourly rates involved, make sure direct costs not absorbed rates.
- If a contract / job is being eliminated, make sure the **contribution** is understood not just use calculated profit. How will the contribution be replaced?
- If a project is being justified by internal efficiency improvements, make sure using the **direct costs,** not absorbed rates.

Beware following comments to justify a proposal:

- It means we do not have to recruit anyone else.
- Make sure anyone talking profit understands what it means.
- Using the discounted cost of money (usually this would be so marginal).
- It's in the budget.
- The customer needs us to do it. Why? Are they paying for it?

BIG SECRET

I have attended countless courses, read many management books and been involved in many campaigns to improve performance. With all these many and various experiences, one thing has come shining through that I have yet to see written in any substantial management textbook.

If you ask people to help and treat them with respect, providing they have clear objectives and support coupled with minimum interference, they will usually produce a good result!

SMALL v. LARGE BUSINESSES
(TASK v. PROCESS)

A large business usually employs a lot of people, and as a consequence the way they all behave has to be more clearly defined in the BUSINESS PROCESSES. A much smaller business usually is more action or TASK focussed. Executives moving between these two types of businesses have to take these differences into account as it could result in a completely different job.

Some differences when moving between these different businesses:

From Large to Small Businesses
Never forget the importance of profit and CASH.
Be direct and visible — you are expected to lead.
Have strong direct relationships with key people.
Do not hide behind process leaders, like HR.
Make sure everyone has a clear understanding of his or her role.
Be prepared to personally coach and mentor.
Leave the politics at the door.

From Small to Large Businesses
Understand why you have been recruited. It's not always obvious.
Map out the process points / control mechanisms of the company.
Form relationships across departments.
Embrace the power of the process leaders and use it.
Delegate time consuming tasks to the administrators.
Note: Being "Bright and Right" can be a distinct advantage.
Relax, go with the flow and enjoy the perks.
Play the politics. It can be fun.

Executives moving from LARGE to a SMALL company often find this difficult as they are usually required to have a broad understanding of the General Management role and have few admin / staff people to turn to for support and advice.

THIS IS IMPORTANT

> If at first you do not succeed, find someone who knows what they are doing!

HOW DO YOU KNOW
Success, just how do you define it?

Using the stakeholder concept of a business, the various parties will define success from different perspectives.

TEAM MEMBERS… Security of employment… good benefits… career development opportunities… good leadership.

CUSTOMERS… Receiving what they want when they want it at the right price with the right quality. Exceed expectations.

SUPPLIERS… Secure relationship… schedule stability… paid on time… low credit risk.

OWNERS / SHAREHOLDERS… Growth.. Share value (EPS) increasing… no borrowing requirement.

Low management maintenance.

BANKS… low risk security… other opportunities to lend safely.

GOVERNMENTS ? REGULATORY BODIES… Not in JAIL!

NOTE
Some of these measures are in conflict with each other.
E.g., Maximum profits and reduced prices. A business judgement issue.

**Did I forget to mention that if you do not meet your targets for
SALES / PROFIT / CASH
*YOU MAY JUST GET FIRED***

A DAY WITH A CEO

CHECK LISTS
A POWERFUL TOOL

CHECK LISTS   A POWERFUL TOOL

Checklists can be used as aides to doing things like the following,

OR

You should also create your own action checklists to monitor
progress and activity.

*I am such a huge fan of check lists that I actually put things on that I have already
done to have the satisfaction of crossing them off!!*

1. GETTING PEOPLE TO CHANGE
2. MOTIVATE THE TEAM
3. SUCCESSFULLY COMMUNICATE IDEAS
4. LEAD AND COMMAND RESPECT
5. STRESS RELIEF
6. NEGOTIATIONS
7. JOB OF A LEADER
8. PROFIT IMPROVEMENT
9. MANAGE BUSINESS FAILURE
10. ACQUISITIONS
11. MANAGING A DISTRESSED BUSINESS
12. DEAL WITH A CASH CRISIS
14. REVIEW CUSTOMERS
15. HANDLE A FIELD PRODUCT FAILURE
16. HIRE GOOD PEOPLE
17. INCREASE OUTPUT / PRODUCTION
18. RUN A MEETING
19. DO A POWER POINT PRESENTATION
20. EMOTIONAL INTELLIGENCE
21. HOW TO WRITE A BUSINESS PLAN
22. FATAL ERRORS THAT CAUSE BUSINESS FAILURE
23. SOLVE A PROBLEM
24. SPEAKING
25. CREATIVE THINKING POINTERS
26. LOOK AFTER YOURSELF
27. MANAGE THE BOSS
28. THINGS WE MAY DO FOR FREE
29. DECISION MAKING
30. PET PEEVES
31. INCREASE PRICES
32. NOT ALWAYS ABOUT MONEY
33. HOW TO GIVE PRAISE
34. HOW TO FIRE SOMEONE

GET PEOPLE TO CHANGE
Start with praise for the person concerned
Mention your own mistakes in area
Talk about the effects of old behavior
Explain the benefits of new behavior
Tell them capable of changing
Make the first part of change easy
Make sure the change means
      no loss of face
Agree targets for changed behavior
Monitor and encourage new behavior
Avoid words. Good and bad. Right or wrong
Perception is a form of reality

MOTIVATE THE TEAM
Be clear about own goals
Inform everyone of theirs
Give the right training
Coach and encourage
Listen to members
Get to know individuals
Incentivize everyone
Be tough when necessary
Give people space to grow
Let them get on with it

SUCCESSFULLY COMMUNICATE IDEAS
Tell it like it is
If you really believe it show it
Listen before you think and speak
Headlines first then whole story
Consistent clear message
If important, face-to-face
Involvement best persuader
Encourage feedback, act on it
Little and often better than long and loud
Communication works when
      things change

LEAD AND COMMAND RESPECT
Passionately believe in your vision
Build a team that shares your vision
Work harder than anyone else
Keep your problems to yourself
Tell team exactly what you expect
      from them
Listen to team. Respect their skills
Keep everyone informed
      and motivated
Give clear orders make sure happen
Share the profits
Very occasionally be ruthless

STRESS RELIEF
Learn to say no
Take exercise
Stay healthy
Meditation / yoga
Take time away to think
Stay professionally detached

Watch what you eat and drink
Avoid alcohol and caffeine
Change routines. Like route to work
Keep your sense of humor
Trust your subconscious
Socialize

NEGOTIATIONS

Do not fall in love with deal
Have a plan
Start early
Define objectives
Understand process
Define walk away position... Stick to it
Teamwork approach
Research other side
Do not get stranded
Build on consensus
Understand where power is
Make sure deal closed

JOB OF A LEADER

Agree strategy
Challenge thinking
Identify success criteria
Prepare plan / measure
Communicate
Select and manage team
Measure and monitor
Tidy up thinking
Recognize and reward
Reality check
Maintain discipline
Achieve objectives
Inspire and motivate
Follow and support
Develop people

PROFIT IMPROVEMENT

Introduce measure... KPIs?
Identify largest variable costs
Monitor and record results
Allocate dedicated teams
Focus on waste
Good to better is better than
    poor to bad
Use Pareto Analysis to identify targets
Ask about grants
Involve everyone special exercises

Offer rewards for savings
Review all pricing
Review customer give aways
Review obsolete balance sheet items
Dispose of redundant assets
Review all accruals prepayments
Look at people costs
Ask finance if received any unallocated cash
Taxation opportunities

MANAGE BUSINESS FAILURE

Face the facts
Realize not end of world
Cut your losses quickly
Try to pay off debts
Protect / support your people

Do not take troubles home
Learn from mistakes
Salvage the best people and ideas
Give yourself a rest
Start again with stronger foundation

ACQUISITIONS

A Potentially Game Changing Event,
But Expensive and Time Consuming With a High Risk.
Chance of Success 50%

Do not fall in love with deal
Stay objective and detached
Check cultural match
Check out major assumptions early
Allocate dedicated resource
Focus on customers
Pay attention to due diligence
Focus on cash flows

Look for off balance sheet liabilities
Assume owner managers will leave
Have an integration plan
Obtain expert opinion if not sure
Have a day one plan
Carry out one year review... Be honest

MANAGING A DISTRESSED BUSINESS
Profit improvement ideas

Elevate all controls to top
Especially cash / CQ sign off
Put in place daily cash reports
Introduce KPIs for key areas
Talk to key people secure services
Talk to banks get support. Stay close
Talk to suppliers secure credit
Reassure customers
Stop recruitment
Drive all past dues / arrears
Bring orders forward
Reduce stock and WIP
Review / sell surplus materials
Review increase prices
Consider pay cuts

Review working arrangement shifts
Reduce / stop overtime
Introduce short-time working
Stop / reduce travel & expenses
Re-deploy surplus manpower
Introduce good communication plan
Collect debtors / receivables
Delay payments / creditors
Talk to credit agencies, reassure them
Look at subcontract work, in-house?
Review all outstanding purchase orders
Talk to owners / shareholders. More cash?
Mothball plant if not used
Review customer credit limits
Introduce short-term forecasts

DEAL WITH A CASH CRISIS

Determine true position
Produce daily / short-term forecasts
Bring all controls to you
Cancel all automatic payments /
    direct debits
Talk to banks be realistic
Dispose of assets / stock
Collect debts / receivables faster
Defer payments intelligently
Stop all discretionary spend (e.g., travel)

REVIEW CUSTOMERS

Acknowledge all customers are not right
Segregate customers into groups
Example: strategic / good / others / x list
Increase prices to poor customers
    aggressively (x list)
Be prepared to lose customers
Put controls in to accept new customers
Do not leave entirely to sales team

HANDLE A FIELD
PRODUCT FAILURE

Be proactive and honest
Take the high road on integrity
Set up a team / room to deal with it
Develop a communication strategy
Establish root cause and act to stop
Wait until dust settles for the post mortem
Get specialist help
Engage the authorities, if required, early
Set up preventative measures
Ask finance team for best way to report

HIRE GOOD PEOPLE

Get personally involved
Make the business attractive to work for
Ask good people to find good people
Involve the team
Do not rely on the HR process. Hijack it
Start with selling the company to them
Close offers quickly and personally

INCREASE OUTPUT /
PRODUCTION

Use subcontract help
Extend overtime / shift patterns
Improve methods
Recruit temporary labor
Rent temporary accommodation
Talk to customers if causing a problem

RUN A MEETING

Check right people attend; no more, no less
Start on time
Start by stating purpose of meeting
Nominate note / minute person
Agree agenda and time line
Venue and format to suit purpose
Quick stand up meetings very effective
Chair to keep process tight
Close down rambling unless a creative event
Finish by asking if everyone satisfied
Read out key actions agreed get agreement
Agree follow up / next meeting, if required

DO A POWER POINT PRESENTATION

Don't unless you really have to
No one listens
Best case is they remember you
were good
And a maximum of
3 points to take away
If you must,
Keep it short
Do not read out the slides

EMOTIONAL INTELLIGENCE

SELF AWARENESS

SELF REGULATION

MOTIVATION

EMPATHY

SOCIAL SKILLS

HOW TO WRITE A BUSINESS PLAN

A series of numbers joined by words
Agree who for, by when, and expectation
Outline agreement of main objectives early
Agree level of detail and time period required
Start with objectives and key assumptions
Define market data driving assumptions
Include financial plan
Include action plan
Define risks and quantify
Get independent objective help if important

FATAL ERRORS THAT CAUSE BUSINESS FAILURE

Forget importance of profit
Not accept personal responsibility
Fail to develop people
Manage everyone the same way
Concentrate on problems not objectives
Not own personal development
Be a buddy not a boss
Fail to set standards
Recognize only top performers
Try to manipulate people
Try to control results not influence thinking

SOLVE A PROBLEM

Define the problem
Analyze root cause. Not symptom
Establish what information must have
Establish what information would
    like to have
Creative evaluation of choices
Evaluate of choices (risk, cost
    probabilities, etc.)
Clarify decisions made
Develop action plan
Define responsibilities / time line / costs
Action / implement
Feedback, check if worked
Get help, if required
Develop a communication plan, if required

SPEAKING

Research the audience
Use three messages
Use body language
Voice is 38% of deal. Vary pitch on points
Dress to give good first impression
Connect with audience
Warm up before. Clear head
Know subject
Believe in yourself
Rehearse
Stress 3 points at end
Humour very powerful if works?

CREATIVE THINKING
POINTERS

Clear normal constraints
Think freely
Do not discard wild ideas
Write everything down
Not assume one right answer
Do not evaluate ideas quickly
Introduce a facilitator. Outsider
Not worry about looking a fool
Use brainstorming
Challenge the obvious / status quo

LOOK AFTER YOURSELF

Introduce stress reducing activities
Stay physically fit
Watch diet
Reduce alcohol, caffeine
Keep knowledge up-to-date
Read and network
Stay sociable and have outside interests
Take a break, clear the head

MANAGE THE BOSS

Understand that you need to?
Work out their management style
The ultimate boss is the customer
Communicate properly and regularly
Identify bosses objectives / values
Focus on loyalty and support
Be assertive about longer-term issues
Communicate your agenda
Think how other people see you
Review actions and issues
Nip conflict in the bud
Talk to each other
Do not go over head. Unless?
Do not be aggressive
Deal with conflict in a controlled way

THINGS WE MAY DO FOR FREE

Telephone support training
Travel to meetings
Quality reports /audits
Carriage
Return goods no charge. Even if no fault
Literature
Reworks / returns / restocking
Technical advice and training
Learn from the airlines!!!

Try and charge wherever possible
100% profit, 100% cash

DECISION MAKING

Do you have to make one? How important?
Grade by quality (of importance)
Grade by acceptance (by team)
Try to achieve a consensus position
Communicate decision clearly
Take time if really important
Do take autocratic decisions if imperative
Be objective
Sometimes not all about money
Gain acceptance of change
Monitor and be prepared to
        change / review
Correct mistakes quickly

PET PEEVES

People who do not format docs
        for printing
People who answer the phone with hello
People who let a phone call jump the line
People who leave long email chains
People who are late
People who abuse junior staff
People who leave rooms in a mess
Managers that abuse power

INCREASE PRICES

Be selective. Customers / products
Introduce minimum quantity order
Introduce minimum price invoice
Charge for extras, freight packaging, etc.
Use price points
Bundle
De-bundle
Target low volume items, high price
Target low value customers, increase prices
Try not to use price to sell. FABS / USPS
Refuse credit notes
Refuse returns
Increase for late payments
Review distribution channels. Lost margin?
Be personally involved
Use pricing specialists
Only use cost as an indicator
Keep engineers away
Small and often. Better than big events
Review history of jobs. Learn and change

NOT ALWAYS ABOUT MONEY
Some Other Priorities

Safety of team members
Integrity of company
Quality and integrity of products
Personal issues of team members
Team morale
Team members welfare
Community support
Charity local and team members
Have fun reward performance

HOW TO FIRE SOMEONE
A Difficult and Often Emotional Area

Keep decision to let go business focused
Keep process to remove person focused
Make sure all processes are sound
Check all legal aspects with HR / lawyer
Become personally involved
Do not hide behind HR
Remember two important points:
  The rest of your team will be watching
  The person going may become
  important. Work for customer?
Therefore, as much as possible be:
  supportive / positive / professional
  friendly / helpful on transition
Take it seriously and personal
It will be a big deal for the person
Avoid becoming macho man

HOW TO GIVE PRAISE
Very Positive Motivator

Do as near event as possible
Not about you
Be personal mention name
Be sincere or not at all
Be specific about what done,
  why good
Go public, let others know
Give something to remember
  (e.g., letter, trophy)

QUESTIONS TO ASK

AND KNOW THE ANSWERS

THE MORE YOU KNOW,
THE MORE YOU REALIZE
WHAT YOU DO NOT KNOW

JUDGE A PERSON BY
THEIR QUESTIONS
NOT THEIR ANSWERS

WHO? WHAT? WHERE? WHEN? HOW? WHY?

ALWAYS GOOD START

ROLL OF QUESTIONS

One of the definitions of an effective Executive that I like is:

"The ability to learn on your feet without appearing to do so."

General Managers usually do not know about every function that they may be responsible for. One of the ways to improve your knowledge is to ask questions. This section is intended to act as a guide to this process.

Most of these questions are closed with numerate answers required.

To discover more about the Executive, use OPEN questions.

DO LISTEN TO THE
ANSWERS
REALLY LISTEN

"A fool can ask a
question that a thousand
wise men cannot answer."
~G. Torriano

QUESTIONS TO ASK *AND KNOW THE ANSWERS*

Reviewing all aspects of a business is a key role of a GM.
These are some of the questions that you should ask the
COMPANY EXECUTIVES.
These questions may also be asked of you by those that overview
your job like a Board of Directors.

ALL LEADERS

Organization charts
People development plans
Biggest issue / problems / opportunity?
Staff turnover
What measurement reports you use? KPIs?
Relationship with you? Their BOSS?
Ideas to improve performance

FINANCE LEADER

Cash flow reports / cash in hand
Review latest numbers
What costing system in use
Any pending write offs / obsolescence due
Ask for Audit management letter
Any major write offs pending
Relationship with Auditors
IT platform
Financial timetable for year / Budget
Variance analysis discussion to budget

SALES LEADER

Incentive scheme and plan
Customer satisfaction reports
Do sales team have non-compete clauses?
Competitors activity
Customer turnover, new customers
Support from OPS and Marketing
Current order book / backlog
Past dues, late orders
Customer complaints log
Estimating? Who responsible for PRICE?

MARKETING LEADER

Marketing objectives for business
Expenditure and how allocated
Agency used
Customer satisfaction reports
Relationship with sales team
Market surveys available
Competitors report
Sales by mix / margin and channel

OPERATIONS LEADER

All efficiency reports see how measured
Late orders / past dues?
Continuous improvement plans / culture
Quality record / stats
Outstanding vacancies / ease of recruitment
Low cost manufacturing strategy
Supply chain, key suppliers
Overtime levels
Average sales / cost per direct
Ratio Directs / Indirects
What costing system in use
Relationship with sales
Forward load v. Capacity
Capacity development plans / strategy

 A DAY WITH A CEO

HR LEADER

Pension plans and cost
Payroll drift per annum
Training policies / programs
Performance review systems
Succession planning
Average cost per employee statistics
People turnover, reasons, reports
Sickness levels
Compensation plans
Key vacancies, how long to fill
Plans to reduce overhead costs
Private health insurance plans / costs
Company car / Expenses policy

QUALITY LEADER

Quality reports, internal and customers
On-time delivery statistics
Any issues with compliance
    authorities, FDA?
Quality systems manual review
Quality accreditation bodies. Audit status
Customer audit status
Quality culture in business
Risk Management plant
Disaster / Business continuity plan

LEGAL LEADER

Any pending legal actions
Expenditure including with external
    lawyers
Relationship with external lawyers
Any issues with internal policies,
    especially HR
Insurance policies up-to-date
Directors and officers liability insurance
Risk management plan?
Compliance issues. Who responsible?

IT / SYSTEMS LEADER

IT platform in use
Development plans
Areas of authority. What is
    in their control?
Relationship with main users
Data backup strategy / Risk management

PROCUREMENT LEADER

Total spend analyzed by suppliers
Policy re single sourcing, any exposure
Average savings from supply base
Process for supplier review
Supply chain strategy. No. of suppliers
Highest risk to business

RESEARCH PRODUCT DEVELOPMENT LEADER

Product development plans launch timetable
Relationship with Marketing and Sales
Customer contact / involvement
Use of outside bodies. E.g., universities

EXTERNAL ADVISORS

EXTERNAL LAWYERS / SPECIALIST ADVISORS

What is role and costs?

Can internal service be increased to reduce costs?

Any legislation on horizon we need to prepare for?

BANKERS

Review funding arrangements

Covenant review, status

How can we obtain cheaper finance?

What is the debt capacity of the business and how measured?

EXTERNAL AUDITORS

Review latest management report

Any going concern issues imminent?

Relationship with company Management / Finance

Policy re staffing audit

Role with internal audit

What can we do to reduce audit fees?

Any impending legislation / Regulation changes?

INVESTOR RELATIONS ADVISORS

What is IR strategy?

Review investor profile

Review any latest investor surveys

Opinion on company imaging, any ideas?

Fees, what can we do to reduce?

KEY PERFORMANCE INDICATORS

THE GOOD THING ABOUT A KPI IS THAT YOU CAN EASILY DEVELOP SPECIFIC ONES YOURSELF

KEY PERFORMANCE INDICATORS

KPIs are powerful weapons to improve performance with
the following advantages.

The presence of information usually improves performance.
People respond and want to do better if they KNOW what is happening.
A KPI can be introduced quickly from local information.
A KPI can be based on non-financial data.

MOST IMPORTANT

You can often ask the person responsible for the performance to produce the KPI
information, thus achieving personal commitment and immediacy of information.

VERY POWERFUL

SALES / PRICING

Sales / customer
Margin / customer
Sales / person
Sales / customer
Margin / customer
Average order size (money or qty.)
No. of orders / day
Orders % of tenders (quotes)
No. of outstanding tenders (quotes)
Average time to respond to tender (quote)
New customers / day (week?)
No. of customer complaints / week
No. credit notes / week
Average value credit note
Average orders / sales person
Selling cost % / sales
Market share %
Debtor (receivables) in days
Returns by value % of sales
Sales by product

Margin % by product
Sales by territory
Margin by territory
Customer quality stats about you
Average cost / sales person
Average bonus /sales person
Bonus (commission) as % sales
Marketing costs / % sales
Total selling costs /% sales
Number of days to prepare a
    tender (quote)

 A DAY WITH A CEO

KEY PERFORMANCE INDICATORS

SUPPLIERS
Past dues in production days
Output / direct person
Overtime % total payroll
On-time delivery
Days credit

PEOPLE
Sales / customer
Sales / person
Directs / indirects
Cost / person
Average cost / recruit

OPERATIONS
Past dues in production days
Output / direct person
Output / production hour
Overtime % total payroll
Direct people / indirect people
Sickness %
Production hours / total hours
Plant down time %
% Orders shipped late
On-time delivery %
Labor turnover %
Average time to fill a vacancy
Efficiency measures (many available)
% Scrap. Items
% Scrap by value
Average batch size
Production hours / total available (24/7)
Direct labor / % sales
Direct material / % sales
Direct costs / % sales
Direct costs / % calculated absorbed rates
Production margin / % sales

THE GOOD THING ABOUT A KPI IS THAT YOU CAN EASILY DEVELOP SPECIFIC ONES YOURSELF

A DAY WITH A CEO

A PROFIT IMPROVEMENT EXERCISE

MAKE

MORE

MONEY

100 + IDEAS TO INCREASE PROFITABILITY

MMM 100 – MAKE MORE MONEY

An exercise to identify areas of
PROFIT IMPROVEMENT

METHODOLOGY

Review and rank the profit improvement ideas on pages 89-98.

Enter a ranking for the most value potential.

Enter another ranking for the ease of achieving.

Select the top ideas.

Develop an action plan for each idea.

Identify appropriate KPIs to monitor.

Go back "do it" and monitor / report.

**USE CHECK LISTS TO HELP WITH THE
THINKING / KPI SELECTION**

MMM Questions & Exercises – Q1

OBTAIN NEW CUSTOMERS 14 28

Questions & Exercises

1. Review all old customers not traded for over 2 years. Why?

2. Talk to existing customers about their competitors

3. Give sales team bonus for new customers

4. Web search of potential / check your website is customer friendly

5. Review distribution channels. Any opportunity to go direct?

6. Appoint international agents / distributors

7. Talk to suppliers identify potential customers

8. Engage external consultants / agencies

MMM Questions & Exercises – Q2

REVIEW EXISTING CUSTOMERS

Questions & Exercises

1. Review customers, produce x list and remove or price out

2. Ask customers if you can add more value to supply

3. Offer to hold inventory on their behalf, at a cost

4. Check if customer is part of group for other opportunities

5. Check if they can sell your products to other markets

6. Look at what you do for free and charge where possible

7. Offer prompt payment discounts

8. Offer retrospective discounts for volume increases

9. Offer to take over some of their operations. Buy capital equipment

10. Constant review of prices

MORE CAN BE LESS

Most businesses try to maximize sales.
Sometimes taking the few worst performing lowest margin
customers out can increase profitability and make the
business much more effective.
Lower sales. Less work. More profit.

MMM Questions & Exercises – Q3

PRICING

Questions & Exercises

1. Produce list of give aways and charge where possible

2. Charge for freight

3. Review price lists and do detailed review and uplift

4. Introduce minimum order quantity

5. Introduce quantity break pricing. Stick to it

6. Charge for re-stocking / returns

7. Charge for late payments

8. Put cost inflation index in contracts

9. Introduce closed job report. Retrospectively invoice extras

10. Review all input costs and charge where increased

11. Remove all % calculations use actual money sums

12. Avoid round figure discounts like 5% or 10%

13. Bundle items and increase overall prices. Go large

14. Double prices for x customers

15. Dramatically increase prices for all nuisance jobs

16. Place small % increase on orders for a reason. Fuel surcharge

17. Introduce / increase cancellation charges

MMM Questions & Exercises – Q4

OPERATIONS ◆ 17 ◆ 8 ◆ 10 ◆ 31 ◆

Questions & Exercises

1. Review scrap records

2. Review potential for outsourcing

3. Introduce a continuous improvement program. Lean Six Sigma?

4. Introduce compulsory shut down periods. Same holidays

5. Review off shore production facilities

6. Review production batches increase if possible

7. If make to order. Look at patterns see if opportunity to build ahead

8. Introduce suggestion scheme. Ask for ideas

9. Look at competitors activities and copy best practice

10. Review all obsolescent material and sell off

11. Lease any surplus space or assets

12. Review all contract costs see if cost effective to bring in-house

13. Ask suppliers to do more at no extra cost. Guarantee volume?

14. Review shift patterns and costs

15. Review overtime costs and who authorises it

16. Cross train team and multi-task

COPYRIGHT BRIAN MOORE *A DAY WITH A CEO*

MMM Questions & Exercises – Q5

SUPPLIERS ◆8◆ ◆10◆ ◆17◆

Questions & Exercises

1. Tell all suppliers you require a price down proposal

2. Analyze number of suppliers. Reduce and rationalize

3. Review all product returns and associated costs. Invoice for them

4. Search Web for alternative suppliers

5. Research low-cost sources

6. Review buyers bonus. Make sure effective and relevant

7. Meet top 10 suppliers and ask them how to reduce prices

8. Review make v. buy policy to see if there is any savings potential

9. Look at payment terms. Extend? Discount prompt payment

10. Run Internet bidding event

11. Request supplier to do more added value services

PEOPLE

Questions & Exercises

1. Introduce KPIs for key people statistics

2. Take out bottom 10% poor performers

3. Review shift patterns / change if overtime dependent

4. Calculate payroll drift and stop it

5. Review vacancies delay recruitment or cancel

6. Renegotiate with providers of services like health care

7. Defer all pay rises 6 months. Longer?

8. Remove senior execs, promote their deputy

9. Place high overtime earners on staff. Fixed pay / higher status

10. Use part-time people reduce total cost / benefits

11. Outsource work, reduce head count

12. Start an apprenticeship scheme

NON PAYROLL

Questions & Exercises

1. Pareto analysis of spend. Increase controls top items

2. Review all invoices without a P.O. Challenge. Refuse to pay

3. Review all redundant assets check book value. Dispose off

4. Change service providers. Energy / phones / catering / cleaning

5. Research grants training, CAPEX. Regional development

6. Research free local government help

7. Review travel and credit cards. Stop or reduce. Use professional service

8. Review IP see if can sell or license / protected

9. Any expertise in team can sell out, not give away?

PROFESSIONAL SERVICES

Questions & Exercises

1. Review auditors charges. Tell them to reduce

2. Ask auditors how could you reduce fees. Internal audit?

3. Pay attention to audit scope and challenge it

4. Review all consultants fees and challenge

5. Put controls in to stop unauthorized use of consultants

6. Review all invoices received without a P.O. Question and challenge

7. Review and challenge legal fees. Even after the event

8. Consider value of recruiting in-house legal staff

9. Review recruitment costs. Reduce

MMM Questions & Exercises – Q9

OTHER CHECK LIST 2

Questions & Exercises

1. Discuss finance / loan structure with banks. Re-negotiate

2. Review alternative sources of cash, e.g., bonds

3. Lease back capital assets to improve cash flow

4. Review payments received that have not been invoiced. Maybe back to profit

5. Ask for a specialist tax review from expert

6. Local authorities may sponsor sales missions / trade shows, provide finance

7. Develop an acquisition strategy

8. Develop a new product strategy / buy IP

9. Use customers to promote your products and services

10. Use press releases to promote company. Reduce advertising

11. Review IP portfolio. Anything to sell? Is the cost to maintain relevant?

MAJOR CONTRACTS

KEY POINTS

- Long game starts with a very structured and strategic negotiation plan.
- Very competitive to win. Watch give aways and make sure small print is friendly.
- Virtually all contracts are late and over run on cost.
- Have a plan to ensure cost over run in your bank as you go.
- Appoint financially literate manager to monitor execution and identify profit potential.
- Balance of power changes after contract awarded.
- Small invoices as you go. Not one big one at the end.

Questions & Exercises

1. Offer to do more at tender stage

2. Make sure cost escalation clause in contract

3. Nominate key account exec to manage. With bonus!

4. Find out who has the power. Level of sign-off

5. Develop a cost improvement plan

6. Charge for extras immediately in small amounts

7. Use power to re-negotiate if possible

8. Have regular finance / extras / cost meetings

9. Monitor cost to complete in great detail

10. Avoid senior exec trade off discussions. Cash in your bank

Printed in Great Britain
by Amazon